TAROT CARDS

An Easy Guide Book to Learning Psychic Tarot Reading

(The Absolute Beginners Guide for Learning the Secrets of Tarot Cards)

Anthony Mayfield

Published by Sharon Lohan

© **Anthony Mayfield**

All Rights Reserved

Tarot Cards: An Easy Guide Book to Learning Psychic Tarot Reading (The Absolute Beginners Guide for Learning the Secrets of Tarot Cards)

ISBN 978-1-990334-67-2

All rights reserved. No part of this guide may be reproduced in any form without permission in writing from the publisher except in the case of brief quotations embodied in critical articles or reviews.

Legal & Disclaimer

The information contained in this book is not designed to replace or take the place of any form of medicine or professional medical advice. The information in this book has been provided for educational and entertainment purposes only.

The information contained in this book has been compiled from sources deemed reliable, and it is accurate to the best of the Author's knowledge; however, the Author cannot guarantee its accuracy and validity and cannot be held liable for any errors or omissions. Changes are periodically made to this book. You must consult your doctor or get professional medical advice before using any of the suggested remedies, techniques, or information in this book.

Upon using the information contained in this book, you agree to hold harmless the Author from and against any damages, costs, and expenses, including any legal fees potentially resulting from the application of any of the information provided by this guide. This disclaimer applies to any damages or injury caused by the use and application, whether directly or indirectly, of any advice or information presented, whether for breach of contract, tort, negligence, personal injury, criminal intent, or under any other cause of action.

You agree to accept all risks of using the information presented inside this book. You need to consult a professional medical practitioner in order to ensure you are both able and healthy enough to participate in this program.

Table of Contents

INTRODUCTION 1

CHAPTER 1: GETTING INSIGHT INTO TAROT READING 2

CHAPTER 2: OVERCOMING COMMON CHALLENGES YOU MAY FACE WHEN STARTING YOUR JOURNEY 5

CHAPTER 3: THE HISTORY OF TAROT CARDS 13

CHAPTER 4: PROLOGUE TO THE STUDY OF THE TAROT 25

CHAPTER 5: GOING DEEP WITH THE MAJOR ARCANA: THE FOOL TO THE WHEEL OF FORTUNE 37

CHAPTER 6: ELEMENTS OF THE TAROT 60

CHAPTER 7: THE MAJOR ARCANA IN DEPTH 69

CHAPTER 8: WANDS 114

CHAPTER 9: TAROT CARDS FOR BEGINNERS 126

CHAPTER 10: INTERESTING FACTS ABOUT TAROT CARDS 133

CHAPTER 11: CONNECTING THE RESULTS FOR A DEFINITE ANSWER 141

CHAPTER 12: WHY THE MAJOR ARCANA IS EXTRA IMPORTANT 144

CHAPTER 13: PENTACLES 152

CHAPTER 14: CREATING YOUR OWN SPREAD 156

CHAPTER 15: HOW TO CONDUCT TAROT READINGS 160

CONCLUSION 164

Introduction

First and foremost I want to thank you for downloading the book, Tarot

In this book you will learn how to read tarot cards. You are going to learn how to lay out the tarot cards into spreads and understand how the different positions in the spread affect the meaning of each card. You will learn all of the card meanings and several different spreads as well as the meaning of each position in each spread.

By the time you finish reading this book you are going to be able to interpret the tarot cards in each of the spreads for anyone who is seeking an answer; you will be a master of tarot.

Thanks again for downloading this book, I hope you enjoy it!

Chapter 1: Getting Insight Into Tarot Reading

Before moving on to discussing how to read tarot cards, it is important to gain insight into what tarot card reading is and how it was introduced.

What Is The Tarot And How It Came Into Being

The tarot refers to a pack of playing cards. Originally, it was referred to as trionfi; its name later changed to tarock and taroxchi. Its use became common from the mid-fifteenth century onwards in different regions of Europe for playing cards, including French tarot and Italian tarocchini.

From the eighteenth century till to-date, tarot has been used for divination by occultists and mystics. Similar to the commonly used playing cards, tarot comprises of four suits. Each of the four suits contains 14 pip cards that are numbered from Ace or one to ten, and it also consists of four face cards: jack, knight, queen and king. In addition to these, the tarocchi comprises of an individual 21 card trump suit, along with another card referred to as the 'fool.' The fool acts as the topmost trump in certain games, and is avoided in some games.

The first ever documented cards were made between around 1430 and about 1450 in Bologna, Ferrara and Milan in Italy when the extra cards containing allegorical illustrations and images were made part of the original four-suit deck. This unique and new pack of cards was known as 'triumph' or 'carte de trionfi.'

Etymology Of The Tarot

The French and English word 'tarot' is derived from the word tarocchi, which is of Italian origin and doesn't have any particular etymology. Its singular form is 'tarocco' which means 'blood orange' in Italian. When its use spread, tarocchi was modified to tarock in German and tarot in French. There are several theories related to its origin, but none of them is related to the occult or divination. According to one theory, it is related to the 'Taro River' located in the northern part of Italy, close to Parma as the tarot game originated from that region. Some sources also state that tarot comes from the word 'turuq' which is of Arabic origin. It means 'ways.'

Now, that you know how tarot started and what the cards were originally used for, let us move on to discussing the major cards.

Chapter 2: Overcoming Common Challenges You May Face When Starting Your Journey

Picking a deck

This is one of the first questions new practicing individuals have on their minds.

For tarot cards, a deck has a little bit more meaning because it has to be one you're comfortable with. You should consider:

The imagery on the cards.

The images vary depending on the manufacturer and illustrator, there are ones where the cards are portrayed clearly, ones with complex images and symbols, and ones that are very simple in their drawings and decorations.

The maker and your emotions.

You should consider, not the brand (so to say), but the intentions of the person that made the cards. Yes, things like intention are hard to know about, but here is where your emotions come in. You should pick a deck that feels right to you. Basically, trust your intuition and pick one that you feel calls to you and feels good.

If you're interested in getting a reading done, or if you're doing one yourself, it is normal to encounter the challenge of understanding the information that is being given to you. Tarot cards give information regarding something that you've asked them or on a general topic. The problem is that we're used to wanting yes or no answers, it is how humans operate. We can be a little lazy and want someone else to make the hard decisions for us.

The answers offered by a tarot deck are more like advice, and you should listen, think, and then use it to make your decision. If you spend some time interpreting each card drawn and their overall message, then keep ruminating their possible meaning you'll probably find some useful advice.

Also, you should understand the meaning of the cards per se. Let's take the fool card, which has a person walking off a cliff. It could mean any number of things, and as you ponder over it, earlier you remember encountering a very drunk friend about to get in his car and drive in his state, when you appear and insists you'll drive. So maybe the fool is walking off because he knows he'll land safely. These connections deepen your comprehension and your relationship with the cards.

People's response

When one takes on a new practice, the people close to you, and maybe even those that aren't, will offer an opinion or pass judgment. When it comes to tarot cards, there are stronger opinions about it because of the common belief that it is evil. This is a case of the just and honest paying for the actions of bad people. If a bad person uses a hammer to hurt people, would you blame the hammer or it's manufacturer for it? The same thing happens with tarot cards. It is a tool, and the way people use it cannot be blamed on the tarot itself or the person that made that particular deck.

However, there is still the fact that most won't understand or simply won't want to understand. How do you continue doing something that people keep on judging you about? The answer is easy. Remember: You are doing this for yourself, not for them. You are the one invested and interested, not them. The one with the deck and doing readings is you, not them. You are not hurting them, and they are not involved at all. In essence, they should not care or be concerned about what you do in your private time. Hence, you shouldn't either.

Mastering your sixth sense

When people want to become tarot readers, the question always arises: Can I do this? Am I suitable for this? The answer to both cases is yes!

Anyone can get a reading, and anyone can do a reading. There are no requisites. The most probable reason for this type of questions is the stereotype that says tarot readers need to be psychic. Being psychic only means that the person is more attuned and has a better understanding of their sixth sense. The sixth sense is a lot like intuition, you receive small pieces of information or feel things when you're doing something or when you're about to do something. Everyone has it. People just need to learn to listen to it and understand the information being delivered. Practice makes perfect, so don't worry. With time you'll develop you sixth sense and might even be called psychic.

Predicting the future

Is this true? No.

The tarot does not predict the future in any way. The problem is the word **predict**. For most people, it has a final feeling to it, like destiny. If someone predicts a woman will be married at thirty-five, she'll think that there is no other option, no other path. That it is inevitable. This inevitability is precisely what the tarot is not about. Think of it more like a book of wisdom. A place to get information from, to use as a reference or consultation guide.

When you ask a question, 'Should I marry this person?' the tarot offers information on the situation. Like the person's intentions for you, the way it will affect you, how you feel about the situation, and other things like that. Within the cards, there may be some suggestions that it could be a bad decision, but that does not mean you shouldn't marry the person, it just means that as things are right now, there are some issues. Perhaps if you talked more, if both changed just a little, if you saw each other in a different way, the problem might resolve itself and then everything would be alright.

General topics are another thing to be careful with. Let's imagine a girl wanted to know about her love life and future family and found out that she'll marry the man of her dreams in ten years, and in ten more they'll have three kids. To interpret this, remember: **you should always read the fine print on contracts, not just the important bits.** The girl in question might deny every single guy waiting for the one the tarot 'predicted' she'd marry. Or she might not want that many kids but accepted it as something that is 'due' to happen. But that is not what the reading said at all.

Marrying in ten years means that you could meet the perfect guy walking to the store one day, become friends for three years, date for three more, break up for a year, get back together, get married for four years, and then get a divorce. Just like having three kids in ten years doesn't specify if a husband is there or not, and it might mean that you'll have an average of one kid every three years, or twins and then another, or triplets.

A lot can happen within that time and you should keep it in mind but go on with your normal life. The things said by a spread are not final and you can choose your own future. The girl could decide to get married before the ten years, and that she and her partner want to have only one kid. Always ponder it for a while, thinking on all the things each card could mean. Don't interpret the answers you get directly and quickly. Keep your mind open.

Chapter 3: The History Of Tarot Cards

Tarot Card Reading has developed as the major and useful asset for forecasts and taking advantage of circumstances with instinctive power. Be that as it may, do you realize the truth was distinctive when they were started? The historical backdrop of tarot cards is as intriguing as the original pictures on the cards. The account of its development is tickling and unfurl the different truth that is as yet covered up in the layers of past.

Tarot cards are one of the most acclaimed strategies for perusing what's to come. They are cherished close by gem ball perusing and palmistry, or palm perusing, as one of the most notorious techniques for fortune telling in the West. Present day tarot cards have 78 cards separated into two significant bunches called arcana, signifying "mystery." There are 22 significant arcana or guaranteed winners and 56 minor arcana cards. These are then separated further into four suits. The four suits of tarot cards are cups, pentacles or coins, wands or fights and swords. Each suit has four court cards: page, knight, sovereign and ruler. Each suit additionally contains one ace card and nine pip cards numbered two through 10.

To any individual who plays current games, this set up sounds rather commonplace. A deck of cards isolated into four particular suits, every one of which has an ace, nine numbered cards and a few face cards. While Pages don't exist in current playing a card game, the ruler and sovereign remain, and the cutting edge jack card could be the substitute for the tarot knight. The comparability between the supernatural tarot deck and the advanced deck of playing cards is obvious. This is on the grounds that tarot cards were initially utilized as playing a card game.

In the mid-fifteenth century, tarot cards were called trionfi, tarocchi and tarock cards. The plans of the cards fluctuated crosswise over Europe as did the suits. Each deck, be that as it may, had four suits included 14 cards. Each suit contained ten pip cards numbered 10 through one or 10 through two with an ace going about as one. Every one of the four suits likewise contained four face cards: a ruler, a sovereign, a knight and a jack, scoundrel or page. Indeed, present day tarot cards are as yet utilized as playing cards in parts of Europe to mess around, for example, Italian tarocchini and French tarot. In English talking nations, be that as it may, tarot cards are utilized solely for divination.

Some advanced clients of tarot cards demand that the cards began in antiquated Egypt or with the Kabbalah, an old, obscure Jewish way of thinking planned for clarifying the connection between a perpetual, interminable and strange Ein Sof, or Infinity, and the human and limited universe of God's creation. In spite of the enthusiasm of the cutting edge mysterious and New Age experts in an antiquated root for tarot cards, there is no genuine proof that tarot cards began sooner than the last long periods of the Middle Ages.

The soonest known arrangement of tarot cards was made in the fourteenth century. The fame of games had taken off after Mamluk game cards were brought to Western Europe from Turkey. The primary tarot cards were likely utilized in a game that got well known in Italy, tarocchi appropriati. In Italian tarocchi appropriati, players were managed arbitrary cards. The players at that point composed ballads about the cards dependent on the topical relationship of the cards.

Another conceivable starting point for tarot cards was to play a game fairly like current connect. Rich Italian families would commission specialists to make hand-painted decks called "cards of triumph," or "carte da trionfi." These cards were set apart with suits of cups, swords, coins and polo sticks and had a court comprising of three guys, one of which was a lord. Later decks joined sovereigns, trump or special cases and the Fool to make a deck of 78 all out cards.

While it might astonish present day individuals who partner tarot cards with divination, black magic and the mysterious, tarot cards in their unique time were viewed as soaked with Christianity. Each card was designed to be shrouded in Christian symbolism. This just started to move after the cards turned out to be progressively connected with and utilized for divination and fortune telling.

The enchanted and otherworldly relationship with tarot cards had put down roots by the mid-eighteenth century and spread outside of Italy. A French essayist, Antoine Court de Gebelin, guaranteed that tarot cards depended on a sacred book composed by antiquated Egyptian clerics. The cards were then brought to Europe by rovers. While this surely gave tarot card fortunes greater believability, tarot cards originate before tramps in Europe, and ethnic vagabonds were not from Africa by any stretch of the imagination.

As time passed, tarot cards turned out to be progressively connected with the mysterious and the advanced French-fit playing card came into significant conspicuousness in English talking nations. The 52 card deck of hearts, jewels, clubs and spades is ostensibly the nearest to the first Mamluk playing card deck that started off European enthusiasm for playing cards in any case. Tarot cards, in any case, kept on being made and utilized. They are as yet utilized as playing cards in parts of Europe today, and the enchanted relationship with tarot cards has just expanded a few people's enthusiasm for them. Accordingly, tarot cards live on in both their unique and progressively otherworldly structures even as present day playing cards rise to be of challenge on them on the two fronts.

Antiquated legend recommends that utilizing tarot for divination purposes began in old Europe. History recommends that antiquated Egyptian ministers concocted tarot cards to speak to their lessons and mystery principles. They are thought to have endure the demolition of the Christian time since book burners were uninformed of what they were.

How a Tarot Deck Compares to a Traditional Deck of Playing Cards

Contrasted with a customary deck of playing a game of cards, with 52 cards and four suits, tarot decks have a trump suit including figurative pictures. The ace in the hole symbolize occasions in an individual's life so it is significant for them to be seen during a perusing. The Major Arcana can uncover occasions, for example, birth, marriage, and passing.

Cups Suit

Cups is a suit that is related with adoration, and satisfaction. It commonly relates to hearts in the present current playing card deck. Cups speaks to the water component, the west course, and the period of fall. Notwithstanding adoration and bliss, Cups is likewise connected with choice, the last phases of life, and different feelings when all is said in done. It speaks to the passionate degree of awareness, and is related with any enthusiastic part of life, for example, marriage and individual concern.

The Swords

The Swords Suit, the suit regularly connected with strife and hardship, ordinarily compares to the suit of spades in the cutting edge deck of playing a game of cards. It speaks to the air component, north heading, and winter season. Other than struggle and setback, it is additionally representative of development, persecution, boldness, desire, hardship, and issue. It speaks to power and mind, thinking, scholarly thinking, and the psychological degree of cognizance.

Wands Suit

In tarot, the Wands Suit regularly relates to clubs, as it connotes action and change. Wands speak to the component of fire, the south heading, and summer. The suit in tarot symbolizes: vitality, development, assurance, quality, instinct, inventiveness, knowledge, and motivation.

The Suit of Coins

The Suit of Coins, relates to the suit of jewels in standard decks. The Suit of Coins may likewise be alluded to as the Suit of Pentacles. The two Pentacles and Coins speak to the earth, the Earth's course, and Spring. Pentacles additionally speak to material belongings, business, security, funds, and exchange.

The Fool Card

A deck of tarot cards regularly has one trick card. Customary playing cards highlight two jokers, which can be contrasted with the trick card. The trick card is thought to speak to the number zero, speaking to the grandiose adventure of the spirit as both the Alpha and Omega, or the start and the end.

Court Cards

Where the conventional deck of playing cards alludes to a Jack, Queen, and King, the Tarot deck alludes to the cards as Knight, Queen, and King. There is an extra card in the court, known as Page. Court cards speak to individuals or parts of an individual. At the point when the court cards speak to physical individuals, they for the most part allude to is possibility that somebody the querent knows or somebody they will meet.

Page Cards

Page cards in the tarot deck speak to youngsters, or grown-ups who resemble kids. Pages are not really youthful, yet might be youthful in connection to another person spoke to in the perusing.

Knights

Knights in the tarot speak to youthful eager grown-ups or youth. Characteristics incorporate life, lack of caution, assurance, energy, and imperativeness. Knights show definitive change, however may unleash ruin as they are incautious and outrageous.

Queens

Queens speak to female power, richness, and maternity. Sovereigns are regularly the principle enthusiastic help for a gathering or family. She holds control close by the King. She has astuteness and want, and knows about how to impact or convince individuals around her. Regularly, the Queen speaks to a grown-up female with a substantial impact in the querent's life frequently speaking to her mom, or a female coach.

Kings

Kings of the tarot deck speak to manly power and authority. The King is somebody who has impact and obligation regarding a whole gathering, regardless of whether it be a family or business. The lord overwhelms, controls, and delegates. The King is likewise profoundly viewed as notwithstanding his capacity and authority, for his ability, information, and shrewdness. For some querents, the King speaks to a dad, or another caring figure.

Tarot is profoundly mind boggling and takes a long time to ace, however is generally prevalent among mystics and those intrigued by the awesome.

Chapter 4: Prologue To The Study Of The Tarot

We are on the eve of a total change of our logical techniques. Realism has given all of us what we can anticipate from it, and inquirers, however, baffled generally speaking, trust in incredible things from what's to come, what's more, are reluctant to invest more energy seeking after the way received in modem days. The investigation has been conveyed, in each part of the information, quite far, furthermore, it has just developed those canals which isolate the sciences.

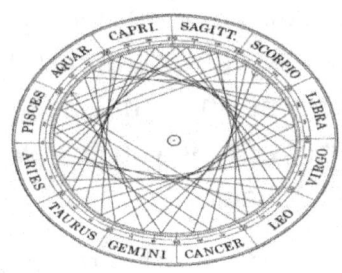

Blend gets important; however, how might we understand it? On the off chance that we would deign to postpone for one minute our confidence in the inconclusive advancement and important prevalence of later ages over the people of yore, we ought to without a moment's delay see that the enormous civic establishments of days of yore had Science, Universities, and Schools.

India and Egypt are even now strewn with significant remains, which uncover to archeologists the presence of this old science. We are in a situation to certify that tire prevailing the character of its instructing was union, which consolidates in a couple of straightforward laws the entire of gained information. In any case, the utilization of union has been as a rule lost, through a few causes, which it is imperative to specify.

Among the people of yore, information was just transmitted to men whose value had been demonstrated by an arrangement of tests. This transmission occurred in the sanctuaries, under the name of Mysteries, and the adroit expected the title of Priest or Initiate.1 This science was hence mystery or mysterious, and hence began the name of Mysterious Science, given by our counterparts to the old blend.

Another purpose behind the constrained dispersion of the high parts of information was the length and trouble of the voyages required before the most significant focuses of inception could become. In any case, as the Initiates found that time was moving toward when their regulations may be lost to mankind, they tried strenuous endeavors to spare the law of amalgamation from blankness.

THE SECRET SOCIETIES

The school of Alexandria was the chief source from which the mystery social orders of the West emerged. Most of the Initiates had taken shelter in the East, and as of late (in 1884), the West found the presence in India, or more all in Tibet, of a mysterious crew, which had, for all intents and purposes, the antiquated union in its trustworthiness.

The Theosophical Society was established with the object of joining Western commencement with Oriental commencement. In any case, we are less keen on the presence of this precept in the East than throughout the entire existence of the advancement of the initiatory social orders in the West. The Gnostic organizations, the Arabs, Alchemists, Templars, Rosicrucians, and ultimately the Freemasons.

The western chain in the transmission of mysterious science. A fast look over the tenets of these affiliations is adequate to demonstrate that the present type of Freemasonry has on the whole lost the implications of those customary images which establish the trust that it should have transmitted through the ages. The intricate ceremonials of the custom seem crazy to the vulgarian. Great feelings of a legal counselor or food merchant, those real modem delegates of the significant principles of days of yore.

We should make a few special cases in support of incredible scholars, as Ragon and a couple of others. To put it plainly, Freemasonry has lost the convention trusted to it, and can't be independent from anyone else, give us the engineered law for which we are looking for.

THE CULTUS

The mystery social orders were intended to transmit in their imagery the logical side of crude inception, and the strict orders were to build up the philosophical what's more, powerful parts of the regulation. Each cleric of an old ideology was one of the Starts; in other words, he knew superbly well that just a single religion existed and that the cultus only served to make an interpretation of this religion to the various countries as per their specific dispositions.

This reality prompted a significant outcome, to be specific, that a cleric, regardless of which of the divine beings he served, got respect in the sanctuaries of the various gods, and was permitted to offer penance to them. However, this situation must not infer any thought of polytheism. The Jewish High Priest in Jerusalem gotten one of the Initiates, Alexander the Great, into the Temple, and drove him into the Holy of Holies, to offer penance.

Our strict debates for the matchless quality of one ideology over another would have made a lot of diversions any of the old start clerics; they were not able assume that insightful men could disregard the solidarity of upset beliefs in a single central religion.

Sectarianism, primarily continued by two statements of faith, similarly blinded by their blunders, the Christian and the Muslim, was the reason for the absolute loss of the mystery teaching, which gave the way to Synthetic Unity. Still more prominent work is required to re-find Synthesis in our Western religions than to discover it in Freemasonry.

The Jews alone had no longer the soul yet the letter of their oral or Kabalistic conventions. The Bible, written in Hebrew, is a brilliant start, for it contains all the mysterious customs, in spite of the fact that its actual sense has never yet been uncovered. Fabre d'Olivet initiated this colossal work, yet the oblivious relatives of the Inquisition at Rome have set such ponders on the rundown of things disallowed.

1 Posterity will judge them. However, every cultus has its custom, its book, its Bible, which train the individuals who realize how to peruse them the solidarity of upset statements of faith, disregarding

the distinction existing in the custom of different nations. The Sepher Beresliith of Moses is the Jewish Bible; the Apocalypse and the Esoteric Gospels structure the Christian Bible; the Legend of Hiram is the Bible of Freemasonry; the Odyssey is the Bible of the purported polytheism of Greece; the Need that of Rome; and ultimately the Hindu Vedas and the Muslims Koran are outstanding to all understudies of old religious philosophy.

To anybody having the key, upset these Bibles uncover a similar convention; however this key, which can open Elusiveness is lost by the sectarians of our Western statements of faith. It is in this way futile to look for it any longer among them.

1 See Fabre d'Olivet, La Langue Hébraïque Restituée.

THE PEOPLE

The Sages were under no figments regarding the conceivable fate of the convention which they trusted to the knowledge and ethics of who and what is to come. Moses had picked a people to transmit through succeeding ages the book which contained all the study of Egypt; however, before Moses, the Hindu Initiates had chosen a country to hand down to the generations of things come to the crude teachings of the extraordinary human advancements of the Atlantides.

The individuals have never disillusioned the desires of the individuals who confided in them. Seeing none of the certainties which they had, they deliberately avoided modifying them in any capacity and treated the least assault made upon them as blasphemy. In this way the Jews have transmitted unblemished to us the letters which structure the Sepher of Moses. Be that as it may, Moses had not tackled the issue as definitively as the Tibetans.

It was an incredible thing to give the individuals a book which it could venerate deferentially, and consistently monitor unblemished; be that as it may, to give it a book which would empower it to live, was however better. The individuals entrusted with the transmission of mysterious precepts from the most punctual ages were the Bohemian or Vagabond race.

THE GYPSIES

The Gypsies have a Bible which has demonstrated their methods for increasing an occupation, for it empowers them to tell fortunes; simultaneously it has been a ceaseless wellspring of entertainment, for it, empowers them to bet. Indeed; the round of cards called the Tarot, which the Wanderers have, is the Bible of Bibles. It is the book of Thoth Hermes Trismegistus, the book of Adam, the book of the crude Revelation of antiquated human advancements.

In this way, while the Freemason, an astute and ethical man has lost the custom; while the cleric, too astute and righteous, has lost his obscurity; the Rover, albeit both oblivious and horrendous, has given us the key which empowers us to clarify every one of the images of the agoras. We should appreciate the shrewdness of the starts, who used bad habits and made it produce increasingly advantageous outcomes than uprightness.

In it, where a man of the individuals just observes a method for beguilement, the scholar will locate the way into a cloud custom. Raymond Lully put together his Ars Magna with respect to the Tarot; Jerome Cardan composed a treatise upon subtlety from the keys of the Tarot.

OUR WORK

We will begin by a starter investigation of the components of the Kabbalah and of numbers. Provided with this information, Ave will clarify the development of the Tarot in the entirety of its subtleties, considering independently every one of the pieces which form our machine, at that point concentrating the activity of these pieces upon one another. Upon this point, Ave will be as unequivocal as conceivable.

We will next touch upon certain applications of the machine, yet upon a couple of just, leaving to the authentic inquirer about crafted by finding others. We must limit our own work to the endowment of a key, in light of an engineered equation; Ave can just supply the execute of work, all together that the individuals who wish for information may utilize it as they like; and Ave feel guaranteed that they will comprehend the utility of our endeavors furthermore, of their own.

Ultimately, we will put forth a valiant effort to clarify the components of divination by the Tarot as rehearsed by the Gypsies. In any case, the individuals who believe that mysterious science ought not to be uncovered must not be excessively furious with us.

Chapter 5: Going Deep With The Major Arcana: The Fool To The Wheel Of Fortune

The Major arcana provide people with an insight of significant events in their lives. This simply implies that if you want to give an accurate reading, you need to be familiar with what each card in this Arcanum signifies.

In this chapter, the focus will be on the Major arcana, and will cover the interpretation from The Fool up until The Wheel of Fortune.

Exercise for familiarizing yourself with the cards

From this section up until all the meanings of the cards in the minor arcana are discussed, it is encouraged that you interact with the cards whenever you study the interpretation of each. Simply take out the cards that will be discussed in each chapter and put the rest in your storage. Stack the cards neatly so that you will be focused on one card at any given time.

As you read the interpretation for each card, remember as much as you can before you go on to the next one. Using your journal, write down any words that come to your mind along with the generally accepted meaning of each card.

Do not feel pressured if you cannot be familiar with the meanings of all cards in one session. Take your time in learning the interpretations so that you can provide a better reading for others.

The Fool

This card is commonly associated with the following positive qualities:

Excitement

Fearlessness

Inventiveness

Joy

New beginnings

Optimism

Spontaneity

Visionary

On the other hand, it can also have any of the following negative associations, namely:

Immaturity

Impulsiveness

Lack of responsibility

Lawlessness

Naivety

Thoughtlessness

If this card is revealed in a reading, the client should be ready to face the unexpected. This is because The Fool generally signifies a new beginning, or it could mean that the client will be involved in a journey that is both fun and exciting. With these "out of the box" events (whether a joyful or trying one), the person being referred to in the reading will become more experienced and gain more knowledge. The presence of The Fool in a reading could also mean that the client will meet an unconventional (albeit one of a kind) person. Lastly, The Fool also tells of the untapped potential that is present in every person.

However, if the card is in the reverse position, it could also mean that the person should "look before they leap". This implies that they should be careful so as to avoid making a "foolish mistake". Its presence in the first position is also a warning sign, as it could mean that they are asking the wrong questions or reasons.

The Magician

This card's positive associations are the following:

Action

Confidence

Individuality

New beginnings

Originality

Potential

Power

Willpower

However, this card can also be associated with the following negative aspects:

Abuse of power

Deception

Indecision

Lack of self-confidence

Trickery

Similar to The Fool, this card is also associated with new beginnings. What makes this card different, though, is that The Magician is an excellent sign that pertains to the coming of new opportunities. It also tells the client how important it is to engage in a new endeavor, and that they will have the initiative and resolve to become successful in whatever it is that they want to engage in. Being associated with the planet

Mercury (messenger of the gods), this implies that they will be able to go through problems without experiencing too much difficulty.

However, the negative factors associated with the card also state that the client has to be careful with the people in whom they'll be placing their trust. This is because The Magician also signifies trickery. Its presence in a spread could also mean that the client currently lack self-confidence and is still indecisive when it comes to certain areas that require them to make a decision.

The High Priestess

If this card is present in a reading, the following positive interpretations can be considered:

Intuitiveness

Mystery

Psychic ability

The divine feminine

Understanding

Wisdom

On the other hand, this card can also have the following negative interpretations:

Emotional insecurity

Hidden opponents or obstacles

Lack of intuitiveness

Secretiveness

The High Priestess is known to be the guardian of secrets. Therefore, if it is included in the reading, it could mean that there is a secret that the client wants to reveal, or that a secret will be revealed. The card also symbolizes the unconscious realm and the person's intuitiveness, and The High Priestess serves as the guide to these inner concepts.

If this card is present in a reading, it is suggesting that the client should start to trust their instincts and be guided by their intuition. It could even suggest that another person will provide them with wise advice. If the client is a man, The High Priestess could signify the woman who is most important to him.

However, taken negatively, The High Priestess could also signify emotional insecurity as well as the temptation of resorting to emotional blackmail. It could also mean that a secret is being kept from them, such as unknown problems or opponents. For men, it could signify a woman who is not a good influence on him.

The Empress

Being associated with the planet Venus and the season of spring, The Empress carries the following positive interpretations:

Artistic ambition

Birth

Fertility

Harmony

Joy

Love

Motherhood

Prosperity

However, its presence in a reading can also imply any of the following negative attributions:

Domestic upheaval

Emotional blackmail

Infertility

Over-protectiveness

Poverty

Suppressed artistic expression

Unwanted pregnancy

The Empress is always welcome in a spread simply because it signifies positive concepts such as love, birth, and prosperity. It can represent real pregnancy (that is, bringing new life), or it can signify that the client will be taking part on any activity that has something to do with nature. It could also mean the start of a creative project.

However, the presence of this card in a reading could also mean that the client or (if a man) a significant woman in their life is being too protective of them. This could even serve as a signal that emotional blackmail may be used in order for the other person to get what they want. It may also be a warning that the client will experience financial worries in the near future. Therefore, they have to carefully manage their money. Lastly, The Empress could also signify an unwanted pregnancy or even infertility.

The Emperor

The following are some of the positive keywords associated with this card:

Achievement

Authority

Consolidation

Discipline

Protection

Provider

Reason

Support

Trustworthy

Willpower

However, this card can also carry the following negative keywords:

Failed ambition

Immaturity

Status-driven

Tyrannical

Untrustworthy

Weakness

The Emperor serves as a sign of honor and achievement. In most cases, it also represents a man with a strong influence (such as the client's father or husband/partner), or could refer to an authority figure such as the client's boss.

These associations could imply that somebody in their life who fits the descriptions above will be there to support them – both in business and personal matters. It could also mean that they will be able to influence other people.

However, it can also mean that the client (if male) or an influential man in their life may abuse their power or use bullying to maneuver the outcome of a situation. It could also refer to failed ambitions, insecurity whenever they're around a person of authority, or an overwhelming desire to improve one's status.

The Hierophant

This card has the following positive associations:

Advice

Conformity

Faith

Identification

Knowledge

Spiritual consolation

Tradition

Wise counsel

However, it also has the following negative associations:

Bad advice

Confusion

Deviousness

Disorderly conduct

Lack of faith

Misinformation

The Hierophant symbolizes the moral law, and signifies a wise advisor or spiritual guide. The card also symbolizes the conventional. Therefore, it implies that the person should consider more of "tried and tested" rather than a fresh approach. While this card may signify a teacher or advisor, it most likely represents moral lessons that the client can learn from the situations that they're currently facing. It could also indicate marriage (or a person's desire for it) or other legal responsibilities.

However, if the card is in a reverse position, it could represent confusion or lack of faith, which could cause disorderly conduct. It could also signify the client as being restricted of action because other people are expecting him/her to conform to their expectations, or the person client does not want to follow the convention.

The Lovers

The positive concepts associated with this card are as follows:

Commitment

Desire

Love

New lover

Physical attraction

Relationships

Sex

On the other hand, this card could also carry the following negative attributions:

Emotional loss

Failed love affair

Indecision

Lust

Moral lapse

Separation

Temptation

The Lovers signifies a new love (not necessarily pertaining to a person) that will surprise the client in the near future. It could also represent "an important decision" that could significantly affect their life. The card also symbolizes choosing between what needs to be done (duty) and what the client wants to do (desires of their heart) - if they take the risk, it could result in emotional fulfillment and happiness; on the other hand, following their duty could result in their life to stay the same.

Unfortunately, The Lovers can also symbolize an unhappy relationship or love affair, but the client is not yet sure as to what choice to make in relation to their situation. The card could also be a warning of a possible intense temptation and unfaithfulness to their morals.

The Chariot

This card can have any of the following positive attributions:

Assertiveness

Change

Good news

Movement

Self-belief

Triumph

However, it can also have the following negative attributions:

Arrogance

Delays

Frustration

Over-inflated ego

Rage

Selfishness

Tyranny

When this card appears in a reading, clients are usually advised to sustain their efforts if ever they are currently facing a struggle; this is because The Chariot is a sign that conflicts will be ending victoriously. It also signals the possibility of unexpected good news and highlights the importance of believing in their abilities. The card also indicates change and travel (since a chariot is a vehicle). It could even mean that they'll be getting the car that they want!

However, The Chariot could also mean that the client or an influential person that they know is being arrogant, selfish, and a bully. It could also mean possible frustrating events, delays on whatever it is that they're expecting, or travel plans that didn't turn out the way they want it to be.

Strength

When this card is part of the spread, the following positive associations can be made:

Compassion

Courage

Fortitude

Patience

Strength

Triumph

Willpower

However, the following negative associations can be drawn from it:

Cowardice

Defeat

Fear

Inertia

Loss of opportunity

The presence of the Strength card does not only refer to physical strength. It also signifies the person's ability to overcome immense pressure and be successful in the end. If health is one area that the client is currently experiencing a problem, this card could represent quick recovery. This is also true if the person is thinking of quitting from unhealthy habits; the card also indicates that it's about time that they start doing so. Strength also indicates success on many things; this also includes internal issues such as overcoming relationship or career problems, or being protected from jealousy and ignorance.

Unfortunately, the card also carries negative associations such as insecurity or giving up because of fear. It could also warn the person that they might miss important opportunities; thus, they should not give up, especially if they think that they're close to accomplishing what they want.

The Hermit

Some of the positive associations with this card are as follows:

Advice

Guidance

Introspection

Patience

Solitude

On the other hand, The Hermit can also have the following negative associations:

Arrogance

Fear

Folly

Impatience

Obstinacy

Suspiciousness

If The Hermit is present in a reading, it could indicate that the person should carefully consider the decisions that they will make on a certain issue. It also suggests the desire of a person for peace and solitude. The Hermit is a warning that a person should not be hasty with their decisions, and that they should also consider the advice of people before they make up their minds. On health concerns, the card also represents a time for rest and recovery.

However, The Hermit can also be attributed with arrogance and stubbornness, being suspicious, and refusing to implement the advice of others even if it is helpful for them. Other negative attributions with this card include impatience (which leads to making bad decisions) and loneliness.

The Wheel of Fortune

The following positive keywords are associated with this card:

Destiny

Good luck

Movement

New cycle

Synchronicity

Vision

It can also be associated with the following negative keywords:

Bad luck (although temporary)

Obstacles

Unpleasant surprises

When this card is shown in the reading, it is a sign of a new phase in the client's life. It could also signify good luck. It is destiny that has brought this new phase, and is not because of individual effort. It is also a sign that their current problem is ending and that they'll be reaping the rewards from all their efforts.

However, having a reversed Wheel of Fortune card signifies the opposite – that is, misfortune or unpleasant situations. However, the person should not lose heart; just like a part of the wheel goes down, it will eventually turn up.

Now that you have learned the meanings of the first half of the major arcana, take your time in learning the associations for each card so that you can provide an accurate interpretation when these are revealed from a person's spread.

Chapter 6: Elements Of The Tarot

A standard tarot deck consists of 78 cards. These cards are divided into the major and the minor arcanas. The word arcana mean '**Profound Secret**'. To the alchemists, the arcana tell us the secrets of nature. The Tarot cards are a collection of secrets that tell us more about our universe.

The Major Arcana

There are 22 cards that form the major arcana of the tarot deck. These are the heart of the deck. Each card symbolizes an aspect of an experience that you might have had either in your past or in your future. These represent the influences that are a part of human nature.

Each of these cards has a name and a number. Some names directly give you the meaning of the card – Strength, Justice and temperance. Other cards personalize the approach that we have towards life or to a situation – the Magician or the Hermit. There are multiple other cards that depict the astronomical bodies like the Sun, Stars and the Moon. These represent situations where we have influences from heavenly bodies.

The cards from the major arcana are special. They bring out reaction from within us that are deep and complex. These cards are always given more importance during a reading. When one of these cards occurs in the reading you know that the situation at hand is not temporary. These cards represent exactly what you feel and all your beliefs and perceptions.

The major arcana are a unit on their own. There are different schemes that have been developed through numerology, astrology and other esoteric sciences that help you understand the human condition in a situation.

Major Arcana Cards

There are 22 cards that fall under the major arcana. This section lists them out and also their importance and how you can interpret them.

The Fool

This card shows that you are spontaneous. It shows that you are ready to take up whatever comes your way but are oblivious to the problems that might crop up because of the same.

The Magician and the High Priestess

The magician is active and depicts your conscious awareness. It can also be interpreted that you are able to take over the world purely through will and power. The high priestess on the other hand depicts your mysterious unconscious. It says that you have a potential that you have not realized yet and have never used before.

The Empress

This card depicts everything that is natural and sensual in the world.

The Emperor

This card depicts the Father. It will show that you are subjected to multiple rules in life.

The Hierophant

This card tells you that you are ready to be educated and that you are ready to join a group of people with whom you are able to identify with.

The Lovers

This card can be interpreted as you being ready to enter into a relationship. He must decide what he should do in order to be in a healthy relationship.

The Chariot

The Chariot depicts your will power and how you wield it to achieve greatness and achieve victory in a situation.

Strength, Judgment and Temperance

These cards depict the names themselves. If these cards arise, it can be interpreted that you are a strong person in any situation and that you take just measures.

Hermit

This card depicts that you are in search of knowledge. This knowledge could be about anything in general.

Wheel of Fortune

This card says that there is going to be a change in your life. It shows that your destiny and fate are about to change based on influences.

Hanged Man

This card says that you have given up or sacrificed a lot in life and that you might have to in the near future as well.

Death

This card does not necessarily imply impending doom. It could be that you have to change your habits. It just means that you will be moving on from a certain path of living into another.

Devil

This card shows that you are ignorant about the surrounding and the situation that you are in.

Tower

This card shows that you will make a revelation about yourself very soon.

Star, Moon and Sun

These astronomical bodies depict the softness, brightness and enlightenment that are related to the moon, stars and the sun respectively.

World

This card depicts that you are contented and happy with yourself and the way your environment is.

Minor Arcana

The Minor Arcana as opposed to the major Arcana talk about the forces that operate our daily lives. It depicts the concerns and emotions that make up the drama in our lives. There are 56 cards in totally. These cards are divided into four suits, just like the cards – Wands, Cups, Swords and Pentacles.

Wands

Wands are the suit that depicts creativity and movement. They are associated with the qualities like enthusiasm, risk – taking and confidence.

Cups

The Cups depict emotion and spirituality. They dig deep and talk about the inner states and relationships.

Swords

The Swords suit depicts intellect and thought. They are directly related to our perception of truth and justice.

Pentacles

The Pentacles depict practicality and material concerns. It indicates that we celebrate any interactions with nature and also enjoy any physical experiences.

Chapter 7: The Major Arcana In Depth

The Fool-0

The general interpretation of this card is that of positive change, newness, innovation, and even purity and innocence. In love, this might be a sign that you are not yet ready for a long commitment, and that the time has not yet come for you to settle down; there are still many experiences for you to have. In work, this can be related to a positive change in position, but which might attract some doubts or lack of confidence from the others. In terms of health, this card is usually associated with a fragile condition, while, in finance, this can be a sign that you should follow your instinct, because a good profit is waiting for you.

The Magician-1

This is a positive card, given the fact that it's usually associated with power, and the ability to make a meaningful change (as in improvement) in your life. You have this power (physically, mentally and spiritually) and this is the right moment to do it.

You should follow your intuition in every area of life (love, workplace and finance). You may also try to enter into a deeper spiritual study of yourself in order to get to know your full potential, which might not have been discovered yet.

The High Priestess-2

On the opposite corner is the High Priestess; this card has "darker" connotations, because it is usually associated with something negative; what is hidden – our concealed unconscious. However, this is important to maintain the balance with the everyday reality – the palpable.

Thus, this is a sign that the seeker must look for double meanings, and mysteries, which can also be shown in your dreams.

Pay attention to the messages that the unconscious tries to send to you. In love, this card tells you that you can follow your instincts. In the other areas, always remember to consider everything from more perspectives.

The Empress-3

This card is usually associated with motherhood, the limitless power of a woman, and even with the mighty nature.

This means stability, an abundance of resources, wisdom, and caring. It can also be interpreted as a proper time for marriage and motherhood (pregnancy).

The Emperor-4

Just like the father figure that we are all used to, this card is a sign of authority, dominance, rule-orientation, domination of the mind over the soul, and self-control.

It can mean that you need these values in your life, and you must take this need into consideration, or that there is already such a person in your proximity, and that you should pay attention to his (her) role in your life.

Be more organized in all the aspects of your life that are not developing as you would like them to.

The Hierophant-5

This card is in connection to the need for spirituality, of knowing that you are doing the right thing, seeking confirmation, and wisdom.

Also, you might feel the need for religious guidance in order to make sure that you are on the right track. And this is precisely what you should do.

Search for a person who represents this sense of correctness, morality, and spiritual knowledge.

In the other areas of life, make sure that, at least for the time being, you follow the rules, stick to the traditional ways, and avoid spontaneous decisions.

The Lovers – 6

The Lovers card. The number associated with The Lovers card is number six.

I tell my students that one easy way to remember this is that six sounds like sex.

Although The Lovers card may indicate a sexual relationship, it may not always mean that.

The Lovers card indicates a relationship, not always a love relationship but a beneficial relationship for both parties, or a partnership.

If you look closely at The Lovers card you may notice a lot of very interesting

symbolism taking place.

To me the number 6 card is a card of love and perfection.

When you come across a six in a reading it generally indicates good fortune, good luck, other people could bring good luck, help from others, cooperation, good news, and helpful people.

The Chariot – 7

The next card is The Chariot card. The number associated with The Chariot card is number seven.

The Chariot card indicates someone who is a strong communicator.

You can see that the messenger is traveling in The Chariot. He has the wisdom of the stars that surround him, and he has a star on his crown area which indicates

an activated crown chakra.

He also has an activated heart area. You have to have an open heart to be able to

obtain higher universal information.

The number seven is always a spiritual number. The Chariot card indicates the Spiritual Messenger.

The Chariot card also represents the Merkabah of the Kabbalah.

The Chariot is a vehicle.

When I see The Chariot card in a spread it indicates to me that a spiritual messenger of truth or a spiritual message of truth is involved, or spiritual truth moving something forward.

The Chariot card can also indicate that personal transformation or awakening is taking place. The Lightbody is being awakened and activated.

This type of activation leads to profound healing and a much greater ability to obtain higher truth and wisdom.

Great Healers and Spiritual Messengers in the world spur others onto their own path of personal awakening. Many people are experiencing some stage of Lightbody

Activation on the planet at this profoundly changing time.

When the Lightbody becomes activated we are no longer bound to a three-dimensional existence, and may experience out-of-body travel during dreamtime and periods of meditation.

This allows us to gain information found in other dimensions.

Strength – 8

The number associated with the Strength card is number eight.

It shows a picture of a woman with a lemniscate or infinity sign above her head. She is taming a lion and calms the wild beast.

To me, the number eight always indicates abundance, fortune and balance.

This woman is a healer. When things are in balance in your life, and in your body, you're healthy.

Eight is the money number. Anytime you get an eight card you're talking about

prosperity, abundance, balance, good health.

Remember, the Higher Arcana cards possess a much stronger influence over the

number on the card than the cards in the Lesser Arcana. It's amplified to a much

higher degree. So the Strength card is a perfect card to get in your reading.

When doing a reading and you're asking about business or wealth and you receive the strength card, you probably will find that you'll be able to achieve your goals. You'll probably find that there will be abundance and wealth for you.

If the question was about health, you will find that you will regain your strength and have good health.

The Strength card also means patience. Learning to have patience can be one of life's hardest lessons. Sometimes learning patience takes time.

In the numbers one through nine, eight is near the end, not at the beginning.

Your power and strength, your patience, and often your wealth or abundance require taking right action and then allowing time to pass in order for these things to manifest in your life.

The Hermit – 9

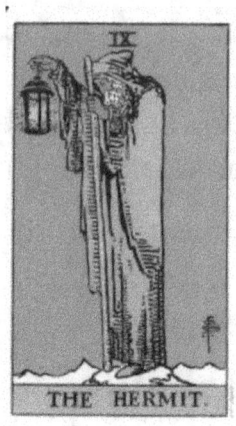

The Hermit card carries the vibration of the number nine, which is the most powerful number.

Knowledge is Power, and the Hermit obtains this power through contemplation.

The Hermit card usually refers to "going within" to obtain the truth or higher knowledge.

When the Yogis retreat to their caves and meditate for long periods of time they often experience an inner awareness of truth that is not as easy to access when living out in the world in everyday life.

When you are able to block out the distractions that we all must deal with, even if only for short periods of time, you may emerge from that retreat feeling refreshed and empowered with knowledge.

We all have the ability to tap into the "Universal Mind" where all knowledge exists.

By retreating into the silence we have a much better chance of perceiving the higher knowledge.

The Hermit is one who has retreated from society. He carries the lantern of

"enlightenment".

When you desire to understand something more deeply it becomes necessary to

withdraw yourself from hurried activities and allow yourself time to ponder and

meditate. It is by "going within" that all is revealed.

Wheel of Fortune – 10

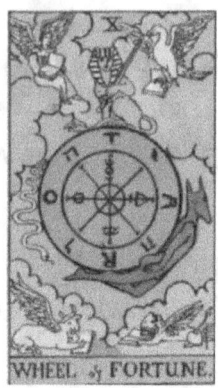

The next card is The Wheel of Fortune card which is associated with the number ten.

As you can see, 10 contains within it numbers that we have already used, which are the numbers 0 through 9. So we can break down the number 10 into 2 parts, a 1 and a 0.

The 0 is a circle and we can see that the Wheel in the card is also a circle. A circle indicates a cycle.

The Wheel of Fortune card indicates 1 cycle having been completed, thus bringing power and reward. Your harvest or good fortune has arrived.

It can also have meaning relating to the Wheel of Karma. The Wheel of Karma's

message is "What goes around, comes around." Another way of putting this is "Do unto others as you would have them do unto you." You see, we always reap what we sow.

When you can truly understand what that means, and can live your life in a way that honors that truth, you will have found real power in your life.

In a reading the Wheel of Fortune card usually represents a completion of a cycle, a clock, time, good fortune through waiting, new cycle, karma, good luck.

Justice – 11

The next card is called Justice and has the number eleven associated with it.

In numerology, you always reduce a number down to a single digit. In the case of the number 11 you would break it down to 1+1 which equals 2.

Remember the number 2 card in the Higher Arcana? It is The High Priestess card.

What similarities do you see between the Justice card and The High Priestess card?

By looking for the similarities between cards, much more of the symbolism is revealed and understood. Always look for the patterns woven throughout the tarot.

In a reading some of the things the Justice cards generally indicates are contracts, legal matters, insurance, balance, fairness, resolution, harmony.

Receiving this card in a reading may indicate that you will be dealing with legal matters or legal documents.

It also may indicate that the outcome of legal matters may be in your favor.

And it can inform you to always work within the light, being as fair as you can to all concerned.

Taking a balanced and fair approach to circumstances will support and empower you.

It can also remind you that "two wrongs don't make a right", so play fair at all costs, even if others around you choose to take short-cuts.

And again, take notice of the symbolism of the two columns and the veil. We've seen that before.

The Hanged Man – 12

The Hanged Man card is numbered twelve.

It shows a man upside down with illumination around his head. He's hanging from a tree. He's hanging by one leg. Observe the symbolism connected with the shape his body is laying in.

The Hanged Man card symbolizes somebody who is willing to release and let go and surrender.

It is often through releasing and letting go that we can, as the old saying goes, "Let go and let God". Sometimes we simply must give up control in a situation.

Sometimes we have no other choice but to accept that we are powerless in a situation.

That is an excellent time to ask for help from the Higher Power and then get out of the way and allow things to unfold in God's time.You must learn, at that point, to trust.

When you receive The Hanged Man card in your reading you need to release and

surrender.

You need to let go of control. You have to release in order to receive.

Did you notice that there is light coming from the Hanged Man's head and he is

illuminated or enlightened?

The tree that he hangs from may be another depiction of the tree of life, or perhaps the cross.

Death – 13

The next card is called Death. The number on the Death card is number thirteen.

We see a knight with a skeleton's face dressed in black riding a white horse. He carries a black flag with a white flower with five petals on it.

He seems to be in black and white although the things behind him seem to have more color in them.

Although he is Death there seems to be a sun rising behind him.

The Death card in a reading indicates death and rebirth.

You must let go of the old to bring in the new. The death card represents a new

beginning.

It can be a very positive card in some cases, although change is often difficult to experience for some people.

The Death card indicates evident change, and also endings and beginnings.

The Death card means ultimate change. It doesn't always mean death in the physical sense. However, when physical death is involved it is not unusual for the Death card to appear.

I must caution you, whenever doing readings for others, it's never a good idea to

predict someone's death. This is one of those times when you really need to be responsible for the power that is being given to you as a Tarot reader.

Some people may take anything that you say, especially something as important as the death of someone, and they may believe it so strongly that it could cause a negative effect on the situation.

When death is imminent because of illness, the other people involved already know it, whether they have admitted it consciously or not.

Your role is not to bring gloom and doom and negativity into somebody's life, but to try to bring upliftment and help to them.

If you sense that there is going to be a physical death around somebody, your best

course of action would be to find a way to gently empower or strengthen the person that you are giving the reading to.

Do not come out and predict death.

Talk to them about learning to connect with the Higher Power through prayer or meditation, if appropriate.

You can gently let them know that all of life has its cycles. And when one cycle is completed a new one begins.

Temperance – 14

The next card is called Temperance. The number associated with Temperance is fourteen.

The Temperance card is beautiful and upon it we see the Holy Archangel Michael.

Michael is a wonderful protector angel. You can see illumination around his head. You can see a round sphere with a dot in the center near the top of this Crown or forehead.

You see a pyramid shape in his heart area. These symbols indicate that he is a vehicle of Higher Love and Higher Wisdom.

Michael holds two cups, pouring liquid from one to the other. Cups, in Tarot symbolism, are symbols of the heart. Water represents emotion or love.

The Angel is standing in water, and he's pouring liquid from one cup to the other or love or emotion from one heart to another.

There's a lot of illumination in this picture as well as water. Michael is surrounded by both Love and Light .

When the Temperance card appears in your reading you can feel that protection is

around the people involved.

And the literal translation for temperance means everything in moderation.

Taking a balanced approach is advised.

The Devil – 15

Number fifteen is The Devil card. The Devil is shackled.

The Devil card generally indicates things in people's lives that have them chained or bound. Those things are usually what we call bad habits.

This can indicate someone's addictions or the things in their lives that are not good for them but that the person has a difficult time changing or letting go of.

These are karmic conditions.

And it may not just be karma from the past. You may be continuing to create more karma in your life that you will have to overcome. There are lessons to be learned here. This is a warning to be wary of people around you who do not have your best interests at heart. It also can indicate that you need to take a look at how your own attitudes or actions are impacting others around you.

This card can also be present if there are situations where being in a jail or prison may be ahead.

Since we are powerful creators, we have the ability to create our own Heaven or Hell right here on earth. Are there things in your life that you must let go of or change now so that you can find freedom?

The Devil card in your reading indicates where challenges or issues need to be faced and overcome in order to move forward.

The Tower – 16

The next card is Number sixteen and it is entitled The Tower.

The Tower card shows an explosion and people bailing from a burning Tower.

We see lightning hitting the tower causing the explosion.

This could be symbolism for the Kundalini within the human energy field been struck by higher energy, but because of blockages in the energy body the higher power has not been able to flow through properly therefore causing an explosion or severe damage.

In less esoteric terms, The Tower card speaks about power being given to someone

when someone is not prepared to receive it.

When power is used or misused by someone who is not prepared to utilize it properly, havoc can ensue. The energy becomes a destructive force rather than a constructive force. This is what the Tower card represents.

The Tower card generally will indicate in a reading that significant changes are taking place. Those changes may not come about easily. There could be destruction involved.

The good news is that we often have to tear down the old house before we can build a brand new mansion on the property.

The Tower can assist in clearing away the old, however, it may not do it in a gentle manner.

We sometimes have to go through periods when we see the old being removed and the sense of loss that goes with it. However, destroying the old is necessary to make way for the new.

There is also symbolism here relating to the Tower of Babel, in which the people could no longer understand one another which lead to chaos and breaking down.

The Star – 17

The next card is The Star and the number for The Star card is seventeen.

As you may know, in using numerology, when we add our numbers together into a single digit we get a clue as to a more precise meaning of things.

17 can be broken down into a 1 plus a 7 which equals eight when added together.

You'll notice that there are eight stars in the sky of The Star card. You'll also notice that the big yellow star has eight points.

All the stars have eight points on them. Eight in numerology is considered a good, positive, prosperous, beautiful number. The Star card to me signifies magnetism.

The Star card will be shown in a reading when somebody has a lot of magnetic energy, when someone is trying to attract a lot of attention, someone who is becoming famous, or someone who already is the star.

The lesson in the Star card is, be careful of what you wish for because you will probably get it.

It means that you have the ability to draw to yourself whatever it is that you desire and whatever it is that you focus on. If you have a burning desire to be famous, to stand out, or to get ahead in this world then there is a perfect chance that it will happen for you if you have The Star card prominent in your reading.

The fame The Star card indicates is not just for a movie star or rock star but also for someone like a famous politician or celebrity.

Any influential person that has a lot of charisma and personal appeal, like a world leader or a spiritual leader, or perhaps someone who has a strong presence and an aura of magnetism about them can be symbolized by The Star card.

These types of people generally use this magnetism to draw to them whatever they want to have or achieve.

When you have that kind of power it can be a double-edged sword. You could have the beautiful things in life drawn to you but if this power is misused then consequences of what you draw to yourself can be severe.

Use this radiant energy wisely.

The Moon – 18

The Moon card is associated with the number eighteen.

1 plus 8 equals 9, and as nine is the largest number between 0 and 9, nine is a power number. It is the largest single digit there is. That creates intensity.

The Moon card, therefore, is a mighty card. Just like the influence that the Moon holds over people, the Moon also has the ability to affect the oceans and the tides.

On the night of the Full Moon, police and hospitals report heightened lunatic behavior occurring. The craziest things happen then. The energy can be intense and wild.

I know that in my Psychic Counseling practice that many people experience heightened emotions during the time of the Full Moon. My phone rings off the hook with people seeking information and help at that time.

The Moon card also suggests mystery, intrigue and things hidden.

It can also indicate that deception is involved. It is a feminine card, as the moon symbolizes female cycles. Moon means month.

The Moon card is the card of the clairvoyant. It tells us to listen to our gut feelings. It talks about feeling rather than thinking. The Moon symbolizes the Mysteries, and all things done in secret or in the shadows.

It also indicates the ability to know the unknown and to see the unseen, and of course the Moon can significantly affect passion and romance.

The Sun – 19

The next card is The Sun and its number is 19. 1 plus 9 equals 10, so you continue to break it down into a single digit. 1 plus 0 equals 1.

The number one is real and focused power. It is also the number of The Magician. It is a masculine number. The Sun is The Christ card. Many religions worship solar deities, of which Christ is one.

The word Sun sounds just like the word Son. Christ is the Son. Another word for Sun is Sol, so The Sun card speaks about and of the soul.

The Sun is the thing that gives life to all things. Life could not be sustained without the Sun. In a reading The Sun card represents blessings, power, birth, goodness, light, joy, strength, success, victory, happiness. The Sun card symbolizes dynamic energy.It is masculine rather than feminine.

It is yang rather than yin. Think of the Sun's powerful rays shooting outward to get a good idea of what this dynamic energy is like.

It sends rather than receives. The Sun is a magnificent, pure, life-giving and life-sustaining force that blesses all that it comes in contact with.

It is a Divine Light.

Judgment – 20

Card number 20 is called Judgement. By the way, that spelling is not a typo. That is the way it was spelled when these cards were initially created.

It's the number 20, the 20 indicating a 2 plus 0 equals the second time around a cycle. 2 equals second. And the zero 0 equals a cycle.

This is another cycle card, and indicates the completion of one cycle and perhaps the beginning of another. On this card we see the Holy Archangel Gabriel.

I have found that this card often shows in a reading when someone is artistic. It is associated with musicians, painters, writers and other heart-opened individuals, the type of people that one might describe as "inspired".

The Judgement card symbolizes rising up again, a rebirth, a renewal, a coming back to life, resurrection.

It also means that there are decisions and judgments to be made.

It is also an opportunity to leave your sins or your karma behind and start a new life, being reborn through the heart, or a second chance.

I firmly believe that this card also indicates a time of Upliftment or Ascension. Many on the planet are experiencing a raising up of vibration or a type of ascension to a higher level of Love, Healing and Awakening.

I would consider this a type of Spiritual Initiation. When you "rise up" or ascend, you are then able to see things from a higher point of view. Your awareness expands. This is taking place on the planet now.

The World – 21

Card number twenty-one is called The World. And we see another circle or cycle. It's really a completion of the cycles. The World card is the highest card of the Higher Arcana of the Tarot. It is the ultimate step on this journey.

However, in a world of Life Everlasting, there is always another, higher level to go to after we have completed this series of lessons.

To me The World card indicates a doorway into the next dimension.

It means that you have traveled through all of life's lessons and hopefully learned them. You must walk a mile in every man's moccasins before you gain true power and ascend to the next level.

The World card indicates that you have doors opening for you, probably because of the lessons that you have learned in this life.

In a reading The World card indicates mastery, wisdom, ascension, blessings,

fulfillment, doors are opening for you and new opportunities, because you have earned it.

It is truly Graduation Day from the School of Life.

You have achieved mastery over the mundane. You have learned the great lessons and worked to develop the great virtues.

You have, through your humility, hard work, and faith become a wise and powerful Master.

Use your power wisely and with great love. I hand you the key of truth and ask only now that you share your blessings with those around you who have not yet walked in your shoes.

Show them all kindness and teach them well, for we truly teach by our actions, and the example we show by living life as though the God in everything and everyone matters.

Chapter 8: Wands

Wands are the suit that depicts creativity and movement. They are associated you're your qualities like enthusiasm, confidence and self – esteem. They also tell you about your risk – taking attitude.

Here are the individual wands explained.

Ace of wands- The ace of wands signifies beginnings and the creation of power. It is meant to imply the potential that one has to inspire new beginnings and see through a change in its status quo. However, it is also prone to delay and a lack of positive motivation in order to plunge in the right direction. The person is weighed down owing to this very aspect.

Two of wands- the two of wands signifies dealing with the future aspect of things. It stands for planning the future and also determines progress. It caters to the decision-making process and leads to discovery. The reverse of this card signifies a difficulty in the process of planning and having a constant fear of what is to come in the future.

Three of wands- The upright three of wands card signifies a person's tendency to remain prepared for any situation and having a foresight. It caters to the person's need for growth and expansion and nature of enterprise. The reversed card signifies a lack of foresight and the difficulties and hurdles that they have to pass in order to attain their goals in life, both long and short.

Four of wands- The four of wands card is considered to be a good card as it signifies the harmony in relationships and the beginning of new ones. It stands for home and community and also foretells an upcoming marriage. The reverse of this card signifies a lack of communication and transition, which might be causing the person some problems in their relationships.

Five of wands- The five of wands card stands for restlessness and internal conflict. There is a fear of competition and also an upright disagreement with someone or something. This card has a negative impact when it is upright. The reversed card signifies an upward increase in a person's goals and their tendency to attain more by overcoming life's challenges.

Six of wands- the six of wands card signifies a person's need for recognition and their victory in their endeavors. It stands for positive progress and their extreme self-confidence. However, the reversed card determines their problem with ego and how they lack confidence in whatever that they do. It also signifies their downfall and how their ego has let them down.

Seven of wands- The upright seven of wands card stands for a challenge and also the competition that is put forth in day to day life. It also stands for perseverance and how much hard work a person is willing to conquer these challenges and emerge as a winner. The reverse of this card signifies easily giving up on something and becoming overwhelmed at the prospect of competition. The person will prefer to remain protected and not take chances.

Eight of wands- the upright eight of wands card signifies thrill and swift movement. It can indicate air travel and speed. Anybody who gets this card is bound to travel and undergo changes. The reversed card signifies delays and not being able to close deals. It also puts forth frustrations in regard to the cancellation of travel plans, which can cause the person to feel overwhelmed and give up all too easily. The reverse card also implies that there are just so many options in front of you that you do not know which ones to choose.

Nine of wands- the nine of wands card signifies a strong sense of courage and a person's determination to this world head on. It is a period of resilience and a person's faith is put to the ultimate test. The reversed card says that the person is paranoid and that he or she is hesitating to move forward in the right direction. It is important for the person to be rational and not rush into anything as that can hurt them immensely.

Ten of wands- the ten of wands card signifies that a person is carrying a heavy load on their shoulders, which is causing them to dwindle a little. But the end goal is in sight and they are walking towards it. There might be intermittent stress but hard work is propelling them into the right direction. But a reversed card signifies that the person is taking on a lot of things at a time and might also be running away from due responsibility.

Page of wands- the page of wands card signifies sense of excitement and the existence of enthusiasm. The person is full of free spirit and is adept to discovering new things in life. The person is keenly interested in broadcasting his or her dreams and aspirations in life. The reversed pages of wands card indicates that your new ventures have not paid off positively and you have suffered considerable losses. It also indicates that you have rushed into something without thinking it through and are now suffering thanks to it. Basically, it signifies that you are immature and not capable of making mature decisions.

Knight of wands- The upright knights of wands card signifies passion and energy and is known to promote success. The mere passion for victory is what fuels this card's holder to prosper in life. However, the reversed card indicates that the person is going to face quite a lot of frustrations and misgivings. The person will be restless and impatient and will not succeed at fulfilling their ambitions.

Queen of wands- the upright queen of wands card signifies power and determination. The person will have no qualms about showcasing his or her power to others. It promotes warmth and a courageous nature. The person will pursue their ambition and make sure they achieve what they set out to have. An upright queen signifies a person being manipulative and trying to alter another person's thinking. The queen tries to usurp someone's property owing to jealousy.

King of wands- The king of wands card signifies a person who is a born leader. He is someone that is a visionary and an entrepreneur. The upright card indicates creativity and a responsible person who pursues their ambition with determination. The reversed card signifies that the person is hasty and makes rash decisions without thinking it through. It means that the person is aggressive and is only suited to undertake brief and interesting endeavors. They are not in it for the long run and are only bothered about short-term results and those things that are of a temporary nature.

Chapter 9: Tarot Cards For Beginners

While tarot cards can pale to play a normal deck, enjoying a whopping seventy-eight different cards, any beginner can get a pack and start practicing if they understand the fundamentals. The cards in the tarot pack can be divided into several categories:

Adapt

Main and smaller Arcanes

Pip Card

Court Documents

Once you understand the different characteristics of any category, reading tarot cards is simply a matter of mixing and matching information.

The most basic distribution of Tarot Cards is between the twenty-two main Arcanes, forty pip cards, and sixteen Court cards. The best way to begin to understand the meaning of each card is to arrange each of the 22 main Arcana in a circle, with the first card in position twelve. From there, looking through the map clockwise, you will be able to follow the path of the soul inevitably passes during its existence.

Around the first circle, then place forty pip cards. It begins with a Pentacles suit, the first twelve-position map depicting the winter solstice. In the position of three, follow the Pentacles suit with a sword suit, indicating the spring equinox. Then place the wand suit in a six-hour position, which means the summer solstice. Finally, it ends with a suite of Cups, starting with the position of the nine and marking the autumn equinox. Just as the rotation of the main Arcana represents a cycle, the rotation of the PIP map demonstrates the movement of the Earth around the sun through the seasons.

Finally, between these two circles, evenly distribute the remaining sixteen Court cards, working from the princess to the king in the seeds that correspond to the outer circle. These maps show different important personalities and how we grow over the years.

In this exercise, it is important to note that just because one card fell into the upper circle or the lower part is not more important than the other. Each card, whether it's major arcana or Minor Arcana, has a very special place in tarot reading.

Each seed in a smaller Arcane has very specific meanings that play an integral role in reading.

Cups: the cups are connected to the water element. Just as water can flow smoothly, be stopped by the dam, or boil and anger in the storm, as well as our emotions. When reading the cards that fall under the cups, it is important to read the procedure from one to ten in an emotional way.

Chopsticks: the chopsticks are attached to the fire element. Fire full of rhythm and movement; it can create and destroy. Therefore, chopsticks are the germ of change and action. Reading this dress, you will see cards that represent the first steps in a new beginning, the creation of our destiny, and cards that tell us that we acted too quickly, without thinking about the future.

Pentacle: Pentacles are associated with the element earth. The Earth is stable, solid, grounded. This is where we build our homes, feed ourselves, and support ourselves. Similarly, these dresses focus on the body and our senses. Whether it's creating a family environment where you feel safe, getting financial security, or taking care of yourself and building a family, all this will be found, if you read the pentacles.

Swords: swords are connected to the air element. We can't live without air, and we can't breathe. However, the air can also take your breath away in an instant. Just as the air can be sharp and pungent, so can the sword. This dress focuses on the intellect. It was said that there is no greater weapon than words, so beware of the warning that this seed can carry in terms of communication with others. It also explores the need for mental clarity and new ideas.

It also takes into account the personalities represented in the court's documents. These cards are incredibly important in reading because they can be directly related to you or someone who is closely related to your situation. Sometimes, it can help us understand who we can turn to for help, or who could hinder our progress.

Princesses: princesses and pages are interchangeable, and your deck will certainly be one or the other, but never both. When you draw a princess, you read about someone who is somehow young. Perhaps they have unfulfilled and unrecognized potential or are, in fact, a child. A princess can mean a student or someone who has just started a new adventure in her life.

Princes: princes are synonymous with Knights in a tarot reading, and again the bridge will have one or the other, but never both. The principles symbolize movement and action; they thirst for progress in life and can often be naively idealistic. People who are read like a prince are warned about actions without thinking because they often jump the gun and assume that everything will work out in the best case. Princes are considered eager in all things and are a generous type of person who is always eager to help others.

Queens are considered caring and intuitive people. They are highly respected and admired and lead inspiration rather than command. The Queen can represent a man or a woman if it is someone who illustrates the above aspects. Often, they are a mature person or a relative-someone with life experience to draw on when offering advice.

Kings represent a person who grew up in his life and is now wise and perfect. Often the person who is represented by this card will feel a great duty and responsibility towards others, placing the needs of friends and family before their own.

After examining the classifications of court cards, seeds, and how to arrange a set of tarot cards in order to trace its history, the meaning of each card should begin to become clear. At this time, a beginner could choose a deck card and give it at least a very simple definition. Once you feel comfortable with this information, consider the numbers from one to ten and finally go through all the main mysterious cards one by one. When you have an understanding of what each number represents, and what the titles of the major arcanes represent, you can then read tarot de Marseille. It will take practice, and sometimes, you may need to refer to the reference table, but slowly and surely understand the concepts that go into the divisions of tarot cards, and everyone can pick up and be a simple and basic tarot reader.

Chapter 10: Interesting Facts About Tarot Cards

Without a doubt, the whole experience of reading tarot cards is very interesting. Whether you believe on tarot cards or not – there is always some level of interest they invoke in you. People have definitely associated a lot of myths and legends to these cards. However, there are is no proof of their authenticity. But, whether these legends or myths are true or not – there is always some level of interest that they offer.

Whenever a person gets his cards read, it offers him a completely new perspective of looking at things. It is just like another opportunity to look at the things that are associated with our lives. There is a different way in which the cards are perceived. Moreover, the perception is highly dependent on how the reader reads the card and communicates the meaning to the seeker. Anyway, there are different scenarios to the complete situation. Every time, you will go and seek a reader, the experience and reading is going to unique. But, the fact remains there that tarot reading is interesting and joyous to both the reader and seeker.

Whether you believe in tarots or not, you can't deny the fact that tarot reading can prove to be a really good idea if you are uncertain about the current situation. This can at least give a clue about the decision that needs to be made. Whether authentic or not, tarot cards do provide you with a really good way of stepping back from the situation and letting your intuition make the decisions.

 A good tarot reader is able to guide you in a very authentic manner. He is just like a therapist who pays really good attention to your problems and lets intuition decide the way forward for you. He bases his guidance on the tarot cards.

In amidst of the above discussion, this chapter of the book features some of the interesting facts about tarot cards that you should know. So, without further delay, let's get started.

There are multiple types of cards present in the deck. However, the reader has to choose the one that draws him the most

Tarot cards are mostly used by those people who are uncertain and would like to make a very important decision in their lives. In most cases, they only guide the person. However, the final decision only lies in that person's hands.

There are 22 cards in the Major Arcana

The cards present in the Major Arcana are a representation of a particular event which is life changing

The Major Arcana consists of cards which are numbered from 0 to 21. Moreover, each card is also associated with a planet/star sign along with keywords. This helps a lot in interpreting the card and using its meaning to help the seeker make a decision.

All the cards in Major Arcana have got a person which represents the card

If you take a look at the cards present in the Major Arcana, you will find that there are animals too. It should be noted that each animal has a different meaning

There are 56 cards in Minor Arcana

In normal playing cards, there is the Joker while in Tarot cards there is a Fool. This is numbered as 0. Moreover, this marks the beginning of the pack.

Each card in the complete deck has a specific meaning. Here, it should be noted that a unique meaning is associated to both the sides of each card. Moreover, the meaning can either be positive or negative.

Just like the playing cards, there are different characters in each suit. A proper analogy can be developed between playing cards and tarot cards in this regard. In explanation, the playing cards have Jack, King, Queen and an ace. On the other hand, the tarot cards have Page,

King, Queen, Knight and Ace. Each one of these cards represent a particular situation. Moreover, they can also represent a trait in personality. There can be different meanings.

As far as the star signs are concerned, we have Air, Earth, Fire and Water while in tarot cards we have Minor Arcana which is consisted of Pentacles (Earth), Cups (Water), Wands (Fire) and Swords (Air)

If you are a beginner then you should go for Major Arcana. This is because of the fact that these cards are much more detailed and easier to understand. In other words they are much simpler to interpret as compared to the Minor Arcana. On top of that, the number of cards in the minor arcana is less. Furthermore, if you are well acquainted with the 22 cards of major arcana then it will be much easier for you to understand the remaining 56 cards.

The different suits present in the minor arcana also have a different meaning. They are associated to different domains of a person's life.

It should be noted that the associated of cups is with relationships and emotions. The purpose of these cards is to highlight the changes that accompany the developments and changes in love life, relationships or family related matters.

The association of pentacles is with money and security. The purpose of these cards s to indicate the developments and changes in your finances, work life and career development.

Swords have an association with the conflicts and intellect. These cards are helpful to indicate the development and changes that are related to the negative areas in an individual's life. These can be delays, arguments, illnesses and success.

If you are interested to learn about motivation and projects based on tarot cards then you better refer to the Wands. These cards tell about the developments and changes in the projects, productivity and goals that are really valuable in your eyes.

As mentioned in the above chapters that there are multiple types of spreads or layouts. It should be noted that each type of spread or layout is associated to a unique situation.

This fact is important to consider that the tarot cards should not be taken 100% seriously. Yes, they can prove to be a guideline while making some important decisions however one should not rely on them solely. Tarot cards should be seen as a source of emotional and spiritual guidance and not as means to take important decisions of life.

It is a common myth that only the owner of the cards can touch it. This is due to the fact that there is a special energy associated with each person. This gets transferred to the cards over a period of time.

The symbols of the tarot cards are thought to possess some magical powers.

However, they mostly help the reader understand the reading.

The tarot cards were brought to Europe by the gypsies. They are responsible for this transference.

Based on the above facts and figures, we hope that you were able to get a really good insight about tarot cards. Moreover, it is also anticipated that you have defined a way forward for yourself.

Tarot cards have a really interesting history. They invoke a sense of curiosity in a person and motivate him to learn even more. Getting your tarot cards read can be a new, unique and intriguing experience for most people. These are definitely a product of centuries of evolution. In tarot cards, you can see a whole new world of various cultures which have influenced them over the years. If someone is interested in the cards, then there are really high chances that he gets immersed in the whole process of knowing more and more about these cards.

Chapter 11: Connecting The Results

For A Definite Answer

Up to this point, we have concentrated on the specific meanings of each card, and the way in which they can be interpreted according to the position in which they are placed (the ten positions of the Celtic Cross in our case). Before moving forward to the actual readings, there is one more thing that needs further explanation, because it can be problematic for some beginners: how to connect each element shown by the cards, in order to create a flowing story from where to take a particular, concise answer to your question?

As surprising as it may seem, there is no single way to do that. Everyone should trust their instincts, and let their inner force guide them to a meaningful interpretation of the reading. Harder to do than to say, isn't it? It is, indeed, especially when you are still in the stage where you have to look through the pages of the book to see what each sign or drawing could possibly refer to. While this is perfectly normal in the beginning, you should try, at least in the Personal Readings (which will be explained in the following chapter), to let your conscious give its own interpretation. And, then, you can adjust the final answer according to the traditional meanings.

Trust the Power of Your Instinct

One way to do that is to use the technique known as stream of consciousness. This term might be familiar to you from the list of literary devices that helped you understand the particular traits of a certain character in a literary work. The technique basically refers to the activity of letting your thoughts flow, without trying to control them in any form. Although it can be more difficult in the beginning, you should say out loud whatever comes to your mind when you see a particular sign or element on a card. Simple words, unfinished sentences, interjections; everything can become useful, when, in the end, you will try to connect them. The idea is to let them flow just like they do in our mind – even when you are not aware of it.

If saying them aloud is not possible (because you don't want others to hear, or for any other reason), then you can try to write them down. However, the activity of writing can limit your thoughts (because, of course, you will not be able to write as fast as you think), and, as a consequence, the ideas can be distorted by your conscious self. After doing this for all the cards, try to look for a connection between them, and the problem/question that you had in mind at the beginning of the reading. Use your intuition, and connect the real with the possible elements. Although it can seem that it doesn't make any sense, trust your instinct, because, in the end, this is the leading power in this art.

Chapter 12: Why The Major Arcana Is Extra Important

Do you for some reason imagine that tarot card numbers within the major arcana are for the purpose of keeping count? Well, whereas that would be sound reasoning, the main reason these cards have numbers is to make you understand the direction each card points towards whenever you pick it. And direction here is in terms of attributes. For instance, what does card number one stand for? What about card number two? And once you know that, you can then combine that with the message read from other cards, even if they be from the minor arcana. If two cards point to the same direction, like say, stability, then the message you are reading gains even more potency and you become more confident about your reading.

In short, the numerology of tarot cards is not something you can take lightly. For your information, numbers themselves have vibrations of their own. And it is these vibrations that strike a chord with your energies as the querent to influence the cards that you pick. If you consider that you also pick cards from the suits of the minor arcana, you can appreciate that you have more than one reading to contend with at any one time. And here is where your major arcana card numbers come in to clear any self doubt.

Your card number can shed more light on earlier readings

Your card number can introduce a new perspective to the whole tarot card reading exercise

It is like the way you open a dictionary to confirm that the meaning of a word you thought you knew is really what you took it to be. And at times, of course, the dictionary could give you an entirely different meaning, which when you put into context gives you the most suitable interpretation. You cannot afford to lose sight of the fact that you are not translating card readings in a vacuum. As a matter of fact, you will often find yourself seeking the help of tarot card readings when you have an issue at hand; things not seeming to go well or anxiety and uncertainties creeping in. So whatever readings you get need to be geared towards addressing your very immediate concerns, whether they are concerns you have openly spoken about or not.

Let us look at the cards you will be dealing with:

0	Fool	8	Strength	16	The Tower
1	Magician	9	The Hermit	17	The Star
2	High Priestess	10	Wheel of Fortune	18	The Moon
3	Empress	11	Justice	19	The Sun
4	Emperor	12	The Hanged	20	Judgment

			Man		
5	Hierophant	13	Death	21	The World
6	The Lovers	14	Temperance		
	The Chariot	15	The Devil		

Earlier on in this book, these symbols have been explained in detail and so the table here is just showing the numbers given to those cards.

What meaning does each numeral bear?

Zero: This number carries the meaning of unity; aspect of limitless or infinite; and even potential in its pure form.

One: This one denotes single mindedness and focus; the aspect of being positive and driven; willpower and independence; and also action.

Two: This number points to communication and partnership as well as choices plus negotiation skills. It is also the number that brings out contrasting elements as well as balance.

Three: Number three brings out matters of intuition and mystery; creativity and advancement; and also versatility and fecundity.

Four: Number four bears the elements of simplicity and practicality. It is also the number for endurance as well as achievement. And it brings out the elements of humility as well as stability.

Five: Not only does number five point to passion and adventure, it also involves motion, travel and expansion in general. It also has the element of being erratic and unpredictable.

Six: Number six carries the admirable qualities of sincerity; sensitivity; dependability and protection. It is also the number that gives you nurturing and growth.

Seventh: Number seven denotes imagination; awareness; and mysticism;

and also understanding and healing. It is the one for perfection too.

Eight: Number eight is the one that tells you there is great possibility for opportunity and abundance. It also points to observation and intention. Still, you will see repetition and infinity in this number.

Nine: Number nine has intellectual power; vision and invention; and it also has influence as well as attainment. It denotes anticipation too.

And you may wish to ask, is that all? And yes, that will be all for good reason. Beyond number nine are 2-digit numbers, and their meaning is deciphered in terms of the single digits.

Here is how it goes for numbers 10 – 22:

First of all, you can be sure of not getting to 22 because already one position has been taken up by the Zero or non-numbered card. Thereafter, when you begin to ponder how to get the meaning of those big numbers, you need to think of two ways:

Add the two digits that make up that number and then pick the meanings already shown for the single digits. An example is making number 12 into the single digit 3, by virtue of 1+2 adding up to 3.

You could pick the last digit of that number and get its meaning. That is the digit you will hear referred to as numerical signifier.

You must have noticed by now that tarot card reading gives you a lot of leeway to do things according to your personal taste. And that is mostly because emphasis falls on your ability to connect with the energies of your cards and not so much the method that you use.

Some Details about the Zero Cards

As you must have noticed, this Zero card bears the fool. And you may wonder who this fool is. You may be surprised to know that this card is not as valueless as its number may deceive. Of course, ancient tarot decks included this card with the image of a beggar or even a vagabond, and it is possible that at the time the card was not given much value. Today, however, things are somewhat different.

Though this card is packed in the major arcana to make 22 cards, fundamentally the card has no alliances; being neither in the major nor the minor arcana. That can explain why there are some decks where this card is just plain without that zero or any other number. And although it is often taken as the lead card in the major arcana, it is put second last by some users – rating as number twenty-one.

Essentially what this zero card number means is that you are on clear grounds ready to get direction. And its meaning is positive in nature.

Chapter 13: Pentacles

Pentacles are another name for diamonds in the original playing deck and they also stand for the element of Earth and their cards are about the material body or possessions.

Ace of Pentacles - Upright: someone who will have a new monetary circumstance, wealth, and a demonstration of great abundance. Reversed: someone who isn't prepared mentally or doesn't plan well, or lost a lucky chance.
Two of Pentacles - Upright: someone who has equality in their life, good time organization, is able to change at will, and knows what their first concern should be. Reversed: someone in monetary disorder and very chaotic and confused.
Three of Pentacles - Upright: someone experiencing first accomplishment with cooperation, association and knowledge. Reversed: someone who ignores skills and doesn't have cooperation.
Four of Pentacles - Upright: strength, discipline, ownership, protection, and

moderation. Reversed: excessively desires, thinks mainly about physical things, and worried about self-protection. Five of Pentacles - Upright: uncertain about oneself, secluded, anxious, financially hurt

Or, losing money. Reversed: someone getting over fiscal or spiritual loss. Six of Pentacles - Upright: someone who is giving, generous, altruistic, successful and affluent. Reversed: greedy, thinks only of themselves and what they can get from people, and owes money to others. Seven of Pentacles - Upright: diligence, perception, someone who will receive gain, money and assets. Reversed: doesn't have long-term perception and will have restricted accomplishments or accolades. Eight of Pentacles - Upright: someone who will begin training and will experience and advantage or captivation about their undertaking. Reversed: someone who is a stickler, always wanting everything perfect, doesn't have a strong desire for success, and can't concentrate.

Nine of Pentacles - Upright: someone who is spontaneous, indulgent and extravagant, and knows how to take care of themselves. Reversed: someone who has had or will have a monetary misfortune, and will over spend in their work.

Ten of Pentacles - Upright: money, possessions gained through someone's death, organization, withdraw from work, and family. Reversed: going through monetary loss, lack of success, and isolation.

Page of Pentacles - Upright: possibility of new employment. Reversed: no gain or advancement due to short term concentration.

Knight of Pentacles - Upright: habit, opposition to change, effectiveness, or precise. Reversed: someone who feels stranded, uninterested, and indifferent.

Queen of Pentacles - Upright: someone who is ordinary, caring, realistic, matter of fact, and protected. Reversed: someone

unstable in work and family obligations.
King of Pentacles - Upright: someone who is safe, in command, strong, prepared, and generous. Reversed: overbearing, brutal and commanding

Chapter 14: Creating Your Own Spread

Sometimes you may come across a question that you or a client may have and you can't seem to find a spread that's really geared toward their inquiry. Therefore, you have to come up with your own spread. This is something that only an advanced tarot reader should do because if the spread is done incorrectly it will give the inquirer bad or wrong advice.

So if you feel that you're advanced, what is the first step to creating your own spread?

Understand the Question

You want the question to be as specific as possible. Get a feel for what the client wants or make a list of what you want out of your own reading. Ask yourself or the client what's worrying them in their life at that moment and is there a specific situation they want an answer to.

Common Questions

You want to start with common questions like:

What do you need to know?

What do you want out of this situation?

What is preventing you from achieving a goal?

What are your strengths and weaknesses?

What are opportunities and challenges you want to overcome?

What do you feel is not in your control?

What do you want to see in your future?

Empowerment Questions

You want to also make your client and yourself feel that there is an answer to these problems. You don't want to just lay them out and then not address them, so ask some of the following questions:

What can you do right now?

How can you bring about a good outcome?

How are you able to overcome an obstacle?

How can you resolve an issue?

Where do you need to focus?

Decide the Layout

Next, you have to figure out your layout. Sometimes you can just put down the card however you feel, but other times you might need to take into consideration what the reading is about. For instance, if the client is at a crossroads with a situation, you should arrange the cards in a cross. If you're looking at past, present, and future, you might want to lay your cards out in a linear pattern. Just go with what feels right.

And that's how you create your own spread! You can use this for clients or even yourself if you feel the need to do a reading. Just go with your instincts. The reason most beginners don't create a custom spread is because you should know most of the other spreads and their general layouts as you can use that knowledge to customize yours.

Chapter 15: How To Conduct Tarot Readings

By this point, you already have tons of knowledge when it comes to tarot cards, tarot spreads, how to read spreads and more. But how do you conduct these tarot readings? Is there something you need to do before the reading starts? Are you doing everything right? Well, let's find out!

A Relaxing Atmosphere

Set the perfect place where it can be relaxing and there are no worries of disturbance. This is not only for the person receiving your readings, this should also be for you. You and the person seeking your help are going to share some many things, you should establish a good mutual respect towards one another. Also, you should be able to really concentrate in order to properly read the tarot cards. So your surroundings or the atmosphere should be peaceful, serene and free of distractions.

Small Additions

Do everything you can to make yourself comfortable and at peace with the place that you chose. If you just can find that perfect spot, then maybe you need to do something first? Some people try purifying their space before anything else, they even try smudging it. Add some gemstones and scented candles all around for a better mood. You can even sit down in one corner and meditate for a short while. There are those who go through a full ritual before they can really start reading, this ritual can include circle casting and calling quarters. Another option is to light a few incense candles and play mellow music in the background.

Use a Cloth

Place a cloth on the surface on where you plan to conduct a reading. The cloth that you will use has two purposes. Practically, it really keeps your tarot cards clean. But on the psychic side, the color of the cloth can affect the card's vibrations. We recommend that you use black, because black does not interfere with other energies. Blue, yellow and purple help with divination and your psychic abilities.

Ask Away

Since they know that they need to tell you about themselves sooner or later. You should ask them questions as you shuffle the deck. Sometimes, tarot cards can be quite difficult to shuffle due to their number and size. It can be really awkward to struggle shuffling as you two wait in silence. That's why you should try breaking the ice and make small talk. An additional tip that you should remember, if a card falls out when you are shuffling, don't put that card back in the deck. There is a reason why that card fell out and it should not be included in your current reading.

Let Them Cut

It's important that you let them carefully cut the cards. Also, remind them that they should think about the question they want to ask while they are cutting the cards.

Next, depending on their question, you should choose what spread you are going to use. As we discussed, there are specific spreads that help numerous problems.

Ask for the Card

This is where the person with a question chooses their cards, a very common sight in movies and film. Take note that the questioner does choose the card, but they should not pick up the deck or really touch the card. Just have them point to the card of their choice.

Look for the Meaning

Now, all you have to do is to interpret the meaning of the cards in the spread. As we said before, these cards are viewed as a whole and their combinations should be discovered.

Conclusion

Thank you again for downloading this book!

I hope this book was able to help you to learn how to read tarot cards.

The next step upon successful completion of this book is to start reading your friends and family before anyone else, then once you are comfortable you will be able to read anyone!

Thank you and good luck!

www.ingramcontent.com/pod-product-compliance
Lightning Source LLC
Chambersburg PA
CBHW071447070526
44578CB00001B/247